To Aoife + Nick,

Congratulations on your engagement!

Something small to help plan your wedding!

♡ Anita, Chris, Oli & Sophia x x

TOP TIPS

FOR

WEDDINGS

TOP TIPS FOR WEDDINGS

An Hachette UK Company
www.hachette.co.uk

Summersdale Publishers Ltd
Part of Octopus Publishing Group Limited
Carmelite House
50 Victoria Embankment
LONDON
EC4Y 0DZ
UK

www.summersdale.com

Printed and bound in Croatia

ISBN: 978-1-78685-492-6

Substantial discounts on bulk quantities of Summersdale books are available to corporations, professional associations and other organisations. For details contact general enquiries: telephone: +44 (0) 1243 771107 or email: enquiries@summersdale.com.

TOP TIPS

FOR

WEDDINGS

VICKY EDWARDS

summersdale

For Peter and Alexandra Phillips,
with love

CONTENTS

INTRODUCTION

Congratulations! The question has been popped and accepted, and now you are preparing to celebrate the happiest day of your life. Planning a wedding is exciting, but to have the day of your dreams – and to get hitched without a hitch – you will need to be resourceful, creative, forward-thinking and flexible, especially when the budget looks in danger of bursting. From booking the venue and the honeymoon to tips for looking your most beautiful and radiant, along with advice on how to create unity and harmony within the wedding party and even how to keep the most impish little attendants quiet during the ceremony, this handy guide offers you wit, wisdom and inspiration in organising all aspects of the big day and beyond. Happy planning and good luck!

GETTING STARTED

Whether it's a spreadsheet or a
notebook, having somewhere to
list all the tasks relating to your
wedding is essential. Tick off
each entry that you accomplish,
and do remember to back up and
save paperless lists regularly.

Here's an idea of what should be on your list:

◆ Budget!
◆ Settle the date/book the venue
◆ Send 'Save the Date' cards
◆ Pick best man and bridesmaids
◆ Invitations/printing (order of service, thank you cards, etc.)
◆ Service (readings, music, etc.)
◆ Catering
◆ Cake
◆ Clothes
◆ Rings
◆ Flowers/decorations
◆ Cars/transport
◆ Local accommodation and taxi list for guests
◆ Gift list
◆ Hen/stag nights
◆ Honeymoon

SETTING THE DATE

◆ If your hearts are set on a particular venue then the date may be dictated by availability. In this case, make a booking enquiry as a matter of priority and work from there.

◆ If you are on a budget, bear in mind that venue hire at weekends is generally more expensive. However, would marrying midweek make it difficult for your guests to attend? Weigh up the pros and cons.

◆ Is there likely to be a clash with any other major family or national event? Consult diaries and schedules before finalising and announcing a date.

◆ Send out 'Save the Date' cards well in advance, giving the most important guests the best chance of being able to attend.

◆ Consider the implications of significant local events. For example, will the annual Armed Forces Day or Pride March pose travel or parking difficulties for guests?

◆ Some dates are more awkward than others: will getting married on a bank holiday, or a day such as Christmas Eve, make it complicated for your nearest and dearest to attend?

◆ Does the date you have in mind leave enough time to save for the wedding and to prepare for it? Do consider the practicalities.

Love recognises no barriers. It jumps hurdles, leaps fences, penetrates walls to arrive at its destination full of hope.

Maya Angelou

BUDGET

◆ Set a realistic figure, contingency fund included, and stick to it. Open a separate 'wedding' account to help you keep tabs on your expenditure.

◆ Be prepared to adjust your budget as you go. If you fall in love with a dress then have it, but accept that you will need to trim costs elsewhere.

◆ Shop around: from venues to veils, costs can vary dramatically. Online shops may provide better discounts and a broader choice, while local suppliers may offer free delivery and a more personal service.

◆ Some things cost more if they are specifically for weddings. Try searching for 'child's party dress' rather than 'bridesmaid's dress', for example.

◆ Wedding insurance is a wise investment – just in case. But check your household policy to see what you may already be covered for before settling on an insurance provider.

◆ Keep your receipts safe, and be sure to confirm everything you book and pay for in writing or digitally so that you have a paper trail.

LOCATION AND VENUE

◆ Unless you have a particular venue in mind, look at as many options as possible in order to compare and contrast. Ask questions and make a note of the answers, so that you can refer back. Your local council should have a list of wedding venues in the area, which should also include basic information such as parking, price and whether a civil or a religious ceremony is possible. Plan your questions ahead to help make decisions quicker and easier.

◆ Accessibility, parking and comfort are all important. Make certain that your venue meets your needs and requirements, as well as those of your guests.

◆ Double up: having the ceremony and the reception at the same venue can be practical and cost-effective. Many hotels are licensed for weddings and often have gardens that give you a natural backdrop for photographs, too. This also helps guests who have to stay over, as they can stay in situ.

◆ If you are having a humanist wedding (a non-religious ceremony), check with your celebrant* to be sure that the venue of your choice is a viable option, especially if it is outdoors – clifftops that may need to be fenced off for safety reasons, for instance.

◆ Whether you decide upon a village hall, a luxury hotel, or anything in between, be sure to read the small print of all contractual agreements. Ask about anything that isn't clear to you.

* A celebrant can conduct a wedding ceremony but they have no legal power to marry a couple – you will need to attend the registry office to complete the legal process for a marriage to be recognised by law.

DON'T FORGET

Creating a hub in which to store all physical wedding-related items early on is extremely useful. By dedicating a box or drawer to all things wedding, you'll be able to find them easily, while minimising the risk of losing anything important. If you use a box, decorate it in pretty paper and you can use it afterwards as a place to store wedding keepsakes, such as cards and copies of your invitations.

Items to keep safe in your matrimonial storage solution:

◆ Fabric swatches and product samples

◆ Business cards, brochures and marketing material for suppliers and service providers

◆ Legal paperwork: passport name-change forms and insurance policy documents

◆ Invoices and receipts for wedding-related purchases and hired items

◆ Invitation acceptance cards

◆ Proof copies of wedding stationery and order of service sheets

◆ Inspirations snipped from magazines

◆ Gifts for bridesmaids and groomsmen

◆ 'To do' lists and schedules.

Marriage is a
commitment – a decision
to do, all through life, that
which will express your
love for one's spouse.

HERMAN H. KIEVAL

DISASTER DODGER

◆ Ask for and accept help. Wedding planning can be stressful and may occasionally feel overwhelming. People love to help with preparations – ask friends and family to lend a hand, as this will lighten your load while uniting your nearest and dearest.

◆ Ask people to do things that play to their strengths and encourage mothers and bridesmaids – or fathers and sons – to bond over specific tasks, such as calligraphy for table place cards, flower arranging at the venue or choosing wine for the wedding breakfast.

◆ Do your best to keep your sense of humour and don't lose sight of the real reasons behind what may sometimes feel like a circus.

Love is not love
Which alters when it
alteration finds,
Or bends with the
remover to remove:
O, no! It is an ever-fixed mark,
That looks on tempests and
is never shaken;
It is the star to every wand'ring bark,
Whose worth's unknown,
although his height be taken.

WILLIAM SHAKESPEARE

YOUR NOTES

....
....
....
....
....
....
....
....
....
....
....
....
....
....
....

YOUR NOTES

....

....

....

....

....

....

....

....

....

....

....

....

....

....

....

....

THE CEREMONY

DO stand on ceremony! Or, if
you don't like pomp and pizazz,
DON'T! It's your choice, but
do remember that the devil is
in the detail. The ceremony is
the most significant element
of your wedding, so make
sure that you have checked
every aspect thoroughly.

TYPES OF CEREMONY

◆ If you and your partner want a religious ceremony, be aware that there are usually criteria that need to be met, so an early chat with your vicar, priest, imam or rabbi is advised.

◆ Civil ceremonies can be personalised, although there are restrictions. Readings and music must all be secular*, for instance.

◆ Humanist (non-religious) ceremonies allow couples to tie the knot at sites that haven't been licensed (beaches, for example) and do not require legal registration. This could be the 'real' ceremony following a wedding abroad or quick civil ceremony.

* Without religious content or connotation.

... to have and to hold
from this day forward;
for better, for worse, for
richer, for poorer,
in sickness and in health,
to love and to cherish,
till death us do part...

THE BOOK OF COMMON PRAYER

RINGS AND THINGS

◆ Wedding rings are not obligatory, so feel free to go ring-less or to have matching tattoos instead.

◆ Do make sure that you get rings correctly sized. Nobody wants the bride knocked off her feet as the groom forces the too-small band on her finger.

◆ Consider the type of metal you want. Gold and platinum are traditional, but cheaper options include silver, tungsten and titanium.

◆ Bespoke rings will take time to create. Make sure that your jeweller is confident that they can fulfil your request in good time.

- Having a family heirloom remodelled is a lovely way to pass on a special piece of jewellery.

- High-street jewellers will offer a wide range of styles and prices, but do look online too. Compare prices and reviews carefully.

- Having the date of your wedding engraved inside your rings means that you will never have the excuse of forgetting your wedding anniversary!

Now join your hands,
and with your hands
your hearts.

WILLIAM SHAKESPEARE

MUSIC

- Do ensure that your choices are appropriate to the venue (no hymns will be permitted in a secular ceremony). Don't organise live music without checking that your venue has the appropriate performance licence.

- Do have a back-up copy of all your music – CDs, memory sticks and computers are not infallible.

- Don't choose tracks that need to be played in full. The average walk down the aisle won't allow for the full version of 'Unchained Melody', for example.

- Do provide lyric sheets or hymn numbers if you want people to sing along.

DECORATIONS

◆ Before buying flower arrangements for the church or venue, ask what – if anything – will already be in place. You may be able to use what is already there.

◆ Flowers for pew ends are pretty, but you could substitute almost anything for these: corn dollies, bows, balloons, paper flowers, wreathes of green foliage – be creative!

◆ Confetti is not always permitted at churches or registry offices. Check with your venue and, if it's a no-go, consider bubble wands, rice or rose petals as possible alternatives.

◆ Remember that the shabbiest of venues can be 'dressed to impress'. Muslin drapes, fairy lights and chair covers can hide a multitude of interior style sins and give a room some va-va-voom.

◆ Bunting is fun, celebratory, and can be easily made. Turn it into a task to enjoy with your nearest and dearest.

◆ Fairy lights add a magical effect and can be festooned everywhere, thanks to compact battery packs. Tea lights and scattered rose petals also look lovely dotted around tables. Even sequins add a twinkle!

A wedding, a great
wedding, is just a blast.
A celebration of romance
and community and
love... What is unfun
about that? Nothing.

ARIEL LEVY

DON'T FORGET

- Consider delivery times and storage facilities for items with a shelf life. Leave delivery as late as possible, but with enough time for you to relax, knowing that everything has arrived.

- Flowers delivered the day before will need to be kept in a cool and dark room to ensure they'll look their absolute best the next day.

- Food also needs appropriate storage. If you are having a cake made with lashings of fresh cream, for instance, check that your venue has a fridge that can accommodate it.

DISASTER DODGER

Appoint someone as your stage manager. Choose a person you know to be organised and reliable, and equip them with:

◆ Telephone contacts for all key members of the wedding party and organisers at the venue/s

◆ A detailed schedule of timings

◆ Back-up copies of all music and texts for readings

◆ A request to double-check that the best man has the rings, the bridesmaids have their posies, the groom has removed the price tag from the soles of his shoes – and indeed anything else that might require a final prompt.

YOUR NOTES

....
....
....
....
....
....
....
....
....
....
....
....
....
....
....
....

YOUR NOTES

....
....
....
....
....
....
....
....
....
....
....
....
....
....

LOOKING THE PART

Wedding attire is a huge industry.
Designer, high street, bespoke
or vintage – decide first and
foremost which avenue of style
you are going to be taking and
then do your homework, ensuring
that you have plenty of choice.

Happily ever after is not a fairy tale. It's a choice.

Fawn Weaver

DRESS AND 'DO

◆ Do try on a range of dresses to get a sense of the most figure-flattering shape for you. Remember to try them on with shoes that have the appropriate heel height.

◆ Don't buy a dress in a smaller size in the hope that you will slim down into it. Buy the right size and have it altered if you need to.

◆ Don't ignore honest feedback. If your bridesmaids suggest that a dress looks bulky at the back then, yes, your bum does look big!

◆ Get your hairdresser to do a trial 'do. Make sure they show you how to make any emergency repairs so you can readjust it yourself during the day.

◆ If you want an 'updo', make sure you have time to grow your hair to a sufficient length.

◆ Don't be tempted to try a dramatically different style or colour too close to the wedding. You don't want your future spouse not to recognise you.

SUITS YOU!

◆ If hiring your wedding suit, be sure to do so in plenty of time.

◆ If you are adhering to any colour scheme, be careful that the shade of your chosen suit isn't going to create a horrendous clash.

◆ If buying off the peg, make sure that trouser and arm lengths are tweaked for a perfect fit (remember to wear your wedding shoes when the trousers are pinned).

◆ Once you have got your suit home, hang it immediately on a good-quality clothes hanger and store in a garment bag.

BRIDESMAIDS AND GROOMSMEN

◆ If you are expecting attendants to pay towards the cost of their clothes, make this clear from the outset. This could save friendships as well as money.

◆ Bear in mind different body shapes, and consider dressing bridesmaids and groomsmen in the same colour, but allowing flexibility with style – subject to approval, of course!

◆ Consider any body art that you would prefer to be concealed when choosing dress styles for bridesmaids.

◆ Don't buy children's clothing too early on or it may be outgrown before the wedding.

A happy marriage is a long conversation which always seems too short.

André Maurois

THEMES AND SCHEMES

Themed weddings can be fun, but be aware that not everyone may share your passion for, say, Harry Potter. If adopting a theme, give guests the option of making a nod to it – Gryffindor colours, perhaps, rather than going the whole Hogwarts. A colour scheme can create a harmonising effect, but do consider shades that suit you, as well as those you like. The two are sometimes poles apart; lime green might be a colour that cheers your heart, but in frock form it may make you look queasy.

DREAM THEMES

Themes that allow for full-on fancy dress or 'just a hint' keep everyone happy. Some ideas include:

◆ Black and white (or another two-colour combo)

◆ Decade-specific (Roaring Twenties or 1960s flower power, for example)

◆ The silver screen (movie-inspired characters or dressed for the Oscars)

◆ Heroes and heroines (St George to Spiderman, Boudicca to Wonder Woman)

◆ Carnival (garlands and colour)

◆ Hearts and flowers (can be achieved through accessories or printed fabrics)

◆ Literary characters (Brontë bridesmaids and Grisham groomsmen!)

◆ Dress UP! (black tie and posh frocks).

Though it rains,
I won't get wet;
I'll use your love
For an umbrella.

TRADITIONAL JAPANESE SONG

DON'T FORGET

◆ Accessories help to make an outfit, so allow plenty of time to source the right bits and bobs. Buy or borrow practical accessories, such as a pashmina for a winter wedding or a lace parasol for a hot summer's day.

◆ Store your complete outfit together, including underwear. Remember to remove labels.

◆ Create an emergency kit for the day, including a spare pair of tights/stockings, needles and threads, safety pins and a hairdresser's cape (or similar) that you can use to protect your dress when touching up make-up.

- If you are going to change after the ceremony, remember to take the garment bag for your wedding dress, as well as boxes for your headdress, jewellery and shoes, so that everything is protected once you disrobe.

- Pack a bag with any changes of clothes that are needed. Make sure someone takes care of your wedding outfit until you return from honeymoon or takes it to your pre-agreed choice of dry cleaner.

- A wedding night demands new nightwear, even if it doesn't stay on for long! Treat yourself to something suitably slinky.

DISASTER DODGER

♦ If you're wearing fake tan, apply it at least two days before your wedding. A bright orange tinge rubbing off on your fabulous dress, especially if it is traditional white, will make you look more brazen babe than blushing bride.

♦ Don't put your dress on until you are otherwise completely ready. Make sure that perfume, body lotion and nail polish are completely dry and, if your dress goes on over your head, keep your made-up face away from the fabric by draping a silk scarf over your face to avoid any smears.

♦ If you have buttons or fastenings that need doing up on your dress, ask the trusted friend or relative who is helping you to wear clean cotton gloves.

◆ Wear a dressing gown over your dress if you are going to touch up your make-up at the last minute and make sure that any small attendants have clean hands. Keep felt tips, paint and sticky jam under lock and key!

◆ Another 'safety first' measure is to drink only clear liquid once you are zipped or buttoned into your dress. Coffee or tea is strictly out of bounds but, as luck would have it, a champagne spillage can usually be mopped up without marking. Cheers!

YOUR NOTES

....
....
....
....
....
....
....
....
....
....
....
....
....
....
....

YOUR NOTES

....

....

....

....

....

....

....

....

....

....

....

....

....

THE CAST

The key players in your special
day will probably be a combination
of friends and family, but do
give really careful thought as
to whom you invite to take on
specific roles – and be clear
about your expectations.

No one has ever
measured, not even
poets, how much the
heart can hold.

ZELDA FITZGERALD

It is written, when
children find true love,
parents find true joy.
Here's to your joy
and ours, from this
day forward.

ANONYMOUS

GIVING AWAY

Traditionally the role of the father giving the bride away was a gesture indicating that the union had parental blessing. In modern times, however, this is sometimes a job taken up by a mother, a stepfather, an uncle or even a son. It really is up to you. Whoever is chosen will walk on the left of the bride and, depending on the style of ceremony, may be required to confirm that they are giving the bride in marriage.

OTHER KEY PLAYERS

Selecting attendants can become political. If your choices have potential to cause ructions, consider how you could give people other roles that still involve them. For example, if you have a particular cousin you don't get on with, and you don't want them to follow you up the aisle, suggest that they do a reading instead. Be diplomatic, but remember that this is your day, so choose people you want rather than those you feel obliged to have.

◆ Whoever is officiating has a significant role in your special day, be it a registrar, vicar or celebrant. Provide this person with some background information so that they can personalise the ceremony – things like how you met and fell in love, what you share together, and your hopes for the future are good basic details to pass on.

◆ For roles such as best man and maid or matron of honour, be sure to choose people you can count on.

◆ Ensure that bridesmaids and groomsmen are fully briefed about their responsibilities and that they all know the running order for the day.

◆ Teeny bridesmaids, flower girls and page boys look cute, but remember that they will need supervising at all times.

GIFTS FOR ATTENDANTS

◆ Gifts don't have to cost a fortune to be thoughtful and personal. Jewellery is often given, with a vast range of possible presents to suit all budgets.

◆ Engraving or embossing can make a gift truly personal. Photograph frames, tankards, pens, books – the choice is endless. Double-check the spelling of names before ordering.

◆ If you are skilled at any particular craft, consider making something. A keen artist might turn his or her hand to creating special keepsake sketches, for example.

- Home-made jam or pickle, or home-brewed beer, is a thoughtful gift. For instance, you could present a flagon of 'Old Matrimony' to the groomsmen.

- Pretty flip-flops for bridesmaids, so that they can take to the dance floor in comfort, will be appreciated.

- For small children, gifts of chocolate, cuddly toys or books go down well. Teenage attendants may appreciate headphones or earbuds (in-ear headphones) in their favourite colour.

- Flowers are a traditional gift for mums, but a planted bowl arrangement is easier to transport and will last longer.

DON'T FORGET

Other roles that can be allocated include the following:

◆ Readers for the ceremony: approach those who you know will do a good job – a clear voice and excellent diction are prerequisites!

◆ Master of ceremonies: if you need to find a role for someone who is comfortable shouting over the crowd then this can be a useful appointment, as they can make announcements as required.

◆ Minister for transport: if one of your friends has a nice car, ask if they will chauffeur the bride or the bridesmaids.

◆ Mary Poppins: if small children will be involved, give someone the job of 'Head Chaperone'. Ask them to have treats and activities lined up.

◆ Hair and make-up assistant: if you have a friend or family member who is good with the brush or the blusher, ask them to be your personal beautician for the day.

◆ Star turns: if any loved ones sing, play an instrument or do a 'turn' of any sort, maybe you could ask them to do a spot during the ceremony or reception?

DISASTER DODGER

If small children are attendants, do have some sort of rehearsal so that they know what to expect. Make sure they understand where they will sit and are aware that being very quiet is really important. Have a plan in place so that any tears or tantrums can be stalled. Non-sticky sweets produced from the mother of the bride's handbag, or a favourite cuddly toy or blankets placed in the front pew or row of seats, are good ways to assure cherubic behaviour.

.There is no remedy for
love but to love more.

HENRY DAVID THOREAU

In our life there is a single colour, as on an artist's palette, which provides the meaning of life and art. It is the colour of love.

Marc Chagall

YOUR NOTES

....
....
....
....
....
....
....
....
....
....
....
....
....
....

YOUR NOTES

....
....
....
....
....
....
....
....
....
....
....
....
....
....

RECORDING
THE DAY

A visual record of your wedding will be a treasured keepsake. Smartphones make it is easy to capture highlights, but be clear about who has access to your lasting memories, and make sure you ask guests to respect your wishes. Include your preference in bold type on your invitation, as well as your order of service, and ask your vicar, registrar or celebrant to reinforce the message before the ceremony begins.

Anybody can be a
great photographer if
they zoom in enough
on what they love.

David Bailey

WEDDING PHOTOGRAPHER

◆ Do look at lots of wedding photography websites, and trawl the albums of recently married friends for inspiration and recommendations. Compare costs and styles.

◆ Don't assume that because Uncle Keith takes great sunset snaps then he can shoot your big day with the same expertise. Wedding photography is a specialist skill.

◆ Do ask photographers for references and testimonials, and make sure you get full quotes, in writing.

◆ Don't ignore your budget. Some camera clubs and colleges will offer photographers who are building their portfolios and so will be cheaper.

◆ Do double up. If you're having a big wedding, consider appointing a photographer who works with an assistant. This will reduce the time it takes to complete the official photos, as one can be setting up the next picture while the other is taking a shot.

◆ Don't be unrealistic. If your fantasy is a sun-soaked wedding on a Caribbean beach but you're getting hitched in the UK in January, retune the mental image. Ask your photographer to find ways to enhance and celebrate the authenticity of your location instead.

VIDEO

- Some photographers also offer video services, but if you want to save money then consider asking a friend or family member who is a confident amateur cameraperson.

- Check in advance with your venue if any copyright issues may arise from filming your ceremony. If marrying in a church, check that filming is permitted. If it is, ensure that the vicar holds a Church Copyright Licence.

- If you don't want guests to film your wedding, make sure this is announced on your invitation and again before the ceremony begins.

There is one thing
the photograph must
contain, the humanity
of the moment.

ROBERT FRANK

SOCIAL MEDIA

◆ Consider using a wedding app, such as WedPics, which guests can join once you give them a password. This enables them to upload their images and you to have access to them.

◆ Let guests know details of any tagging that you would like them to use – #OurFabulousWedding.

◆ Ensure that pictures featuring any children are only shared with the blessing of the parents. Also, never mention other people's kids by name on social media.

PHOTO BOOTHS

◆ As well as being great fun and perfect for capturing happy pictures, photo booths double as entertainment, with guests of all ages able to join in the fun.

◆ Some photo booths provide a 'snap and sign' picture and guestbook service, which could eliminate the need for a separate guestbook.

◆ Prices vary, as do the services included. Shop around and seek recommendations. If your budget won't stretch, make your own booth. Cut out a big cardboard frame, decorate it and provide a box of props, hats and accessories.

Love is life.
And if you miss
love, you miss life.

Leo Buscaglia

DON'T FORGET

◆ Think carefully about which elements of the day you want photographed and how this will affect your budget. Do you want to be papped while you're having your hair done or putting your garter on, for instance?

◆ Your photographer is the expert. Do ask for advice and ideas.

◆ Agree a plan B in the event of bad weather. You might have wanted a group shot outside, but if it's blowing a force-ten gale then you'll need to rethink, which can easily be done in advance.

◆ Do give your photographer a list of shots/people that you definitely want captured.

◆ Colour, black-and-white or a mix of both? Be sure to stipulate your preference.

◆ Ask guests to take lots of photographs. Some of the most treasured memories are relaxed snaps. You could even go old school and put disposable cameras on the tables!

◆ Ask one of your bridesmaids to carry a bag with your make-up and a hand mirror so that you can quickly check your appearance between photos.

◆ Add photo frames to your wedding gift list. You'll have plenty to fill them with!

Photography is a way
of feeling, of touching,
of loving. What you
have caught on film
is captured forever.

AARON SISKIND

DISASTER DODGER

Make sure that someone, apart from the official photographer, brings a decent camera and takes some formal shots. In the unlikely event of a problem occurring with the 'real' pictures, you will have an alternative. Ask a friend or family member who is a keen photographer to take on this job, making it clear that they're not under pressure, but that you would be relieved to know that there is a 'just in case' if your photographer is taken ill or leaves the lens cap on.

YOUR NOTES

....

....

....

....

....

....

....

....

....

....

....

....

....

....

YOUR NOTES

....

....

....

....

....

....

....

....

....

....

....

....

....

....

THE RECEPTION

As a celebration of your marriage, whether you are observing formality or going with the flow, your reception should be a joyous occasion, with plenty of feasting and laughter shared with those you hold dearest. Enjoy it, but be sure to eat before you get too stuck into the champagne!

SIZE AND SCALE

The first thing you must decide on for your reception: is it to be small with a select few, followed by an evening party, or a lavish lunch for hundreds? Get your numbers nailed, first and foremost.

SEATING PLANS

You don't have to have a seating plan, but if you do, there are some guidelines that are worth noting:

◆ Try to avoid separating families with young children and couples.

◆ Be mindful of politics and personal histories. Don't seat people together if you know that they don't get along or have awkward relationships.

◆ Try to sit together people who are likely to have something in common to kick-start the conversation.

◆ Don't forget to include yourself and your future spouse in the plan – preferably on the same table!

CATERING AND MENUS

◆ The wedding breakfast menu is dictated by the time of day, despite its name. A morning wedding could suit a hearty brunch or early lunch, while afternoon suggests high tea. The time of year is also relevant – in December, sausage and mash may be more welcome than salmon roulade.

◆ Buffet or table service?

◆ Make sure you check for particular dietary requirements on your invitation. If you are inviting children, include some child-friendly dishes.

◆ Think about a 'for later' addition like bacon butties or pizza, especially if you are inviting extra people in the evening.

It is such a happiness
when good people
get together – and
they always do.

JANE AUSTEN

DRINKS

◆ Will you have a cash bar at any point? If you are hiring a hall and intend to run a cash bar, you will need to apply for a licence from your local council.

◆ Champagne or sparkling wine for the toast? Prosecco is a very good (and cheaper) option.

◆ Not everyone will want, or be able, to drink alcohol. Make sure there is a good selection of soft drinks available for teetotal guests, drivers and children. A cup of tea or coffee after the meal is always welcome.

Drink to me only
with thine eyes.

Ben Jonson

CAKE

◆ If you want something special, seek recommendations and book well in advance.

◆ If you are a keen baker, why not make your own cake?

◆ If the three tiers of fruit, marzipan and royal icing option isn't for you, go all out with a tower of profiteroles or an enormous Victoria sponge instead.

◆ You could make your 'pudding' the cake. Some brides have a giant pavlova surrounded by mini pavlovas, one for each guest, while others opt for several tiers of whole cheeses, served with biscuits and grapes.

MUSIC

Music at your reception can be divided into two parts, with a solo instrumentalist playing during the meal and then, later, a band or a disco. Alternatively – and increasingly popular – couples are compiling their own playlists, making their music incredibly personal. However, it is worth keeping in mind that people will want to dance at some stage, so choose music that includes an up-tempo, get-your-groove-on section. If you are having a first dance, make sure that you have the track or that your DJ has the exact version you have chosen.

Life is one grand, sweet song, so start the music.

Ronald Reagan

There is only one
happiness in life, to
love and be loved.

George Sand

WEDDING FAVOURS

Sugared almonds are traditional (five of them, denoting health, wealth, happiness, children and a long life) but people are now being much more creative. Here are some ideas for alternative favours, many of which can be personalised with the names of the happy couple and the date:

- Love Heart sweets
- Chocolates
- Sticks of rock
- Miniature jars of honey
- Charity silk flowers, brooches or ribbons
- Lottery scratch cards
- Packets of flower seeds
- Heart-shaped magnets
- Miniature bottles of wine
- Fortune cookies
- Lavender bags
- Candles

GUESTBOOK

If you are having a guestbook then do let guests know where it is and encourage them to sign it. This is something that could also be included in your invitation so that, if they wish, your guests have time to think of something particular to write. Make sure you provide pens (that don't smudge or leak) and leave a written instruction with your guestbook, indicating how many signatures/messages you want per page. Don't leave your guestbook on a bar or anywhere where drinks or food could be easily spilled on it.

DON'T FORGET

◆ Provide a vestibule for people to leave coats, bags and umbrellas, and have a table or designated area where they can leave gifts and cards.

◆ Signage for lavatories is very helpful. Hotel facilities are usually well signposted, but if you are hiring a hall, make sure you add some visual pointers.

◆ Make someone responsible for checking the room at the end to ensure that nothing has been left behind and that any lost property is rounded up.

DISASTER DODGER

When looking at venues for your reception, do bear in mind the size of your wedding dress. If you are going for a monster meringue then everything from door frames to staircases will be obstacles. Specifically, look at the size of the lavatory cubicles and bear in mind that some brides have needed to use the disabled loo, as this was the only one big enough to accommodate their enormous frock, plus the two bridesmaids required to hold it up. What you might call a wee difficulty…

YOUR NOTES

YOUR NOTES

SPEECHES

As well as being a lovely opportunity to share heartfelt thoughts and a few jokes with your nearest and dearest, the speeches also provide a platform for you to publicly thank people. Be sure not to miss anyone out!

I'm no expert standing at a podium giving speeches. I share heartbeats. Compassion.

Elizabeth Berkley

TRADITIONS

◆ Speeches traditionally start with the father of the bride. He should thank everyone for coming, compliment the bride, welcome her new husband to the family and propose a toast to the newlyweds.

◆ The groom thanks both sets of parents, the guests for their presence and their presents, and then the bridesmaids (he proposes a toast to them).

◆ The best man follows. He talks about the newlyweds, especially the groom. He reads messages from absent guests and toasts the couple, and is traditionally the 'funny man' of this part of the day.

◆ Other speeches and toasts may follow in any order.

Chains do not hold a marriage together. It is threads, hundreds of tiny threads, which sew people together through the years. That is what makes a marriage last.

SIMONE SIGNORET

DOS AND DON'TS

- Do encourage those giving speeches to speak from the heart. Ensure they make the appropriate thank yous: sincerity, not waffle!

- Don't leave speeches until too late in the day. After people have eaten and before the drink flows too readily is the ideal time.

- Do let girl power prevail. There's no reason why the bride, the mother of the bride or the chief bridesmaid can't say a few words too.

- Don't let speech-givers make jokes or use language that may cause offence. Be clear about where the line is and choose your best man wisely – avoid those prone to drinking too much and those who would rather face a firing squad than speak in public.

◆ Don't let speakers ramble. On the whole, less is more when it comes to wedding speeches. Give timing guidelines and encourage speakers to leave them wanting more!

◆ Do confront nerves. If you know that your best man has difficulty with public speaking, hook him up with a professional coach who can boost his confidence and show him helpful techniques.

◆ Don't let people wander around or clear tables while the speeches are happening. Ask your best man or master of ceremonies to give a ten-minute warning, telling people to be ready to sit, listen and pay attention.

The very best impromptu speeches are the ones written well in advance.

Ruth Gordon

DON'T FORGET

◆ If speakers need a microphone, ask your venue whether they can provide one. If they can't, consider hiring a small PA system.

◆ Enquire whether speakers may have a rehearsal in advance. Hearing your own voice can be a little daunting, especially if you aren't used to speaking publicly.

◆ If a microphone is not needed, speech-givers will still have to project their voices and look up in order to be properly heard. Remind them that practice makes perfect!

There's nothing
more admirable than
when two people who
see eye to eye keep
house as man and
wife, confounding
their enemies and
delighting their friends.

HOMER

DISASTER DODGER

Emotion can take over, and even the most self-possessed people have been known to become overwhelmed and reduced to tears when giving their speech. Suggest that all speeches are typed up: in the event of someone being unable to continue, another can step into the breach to read the rest, without having to negotiate scrappy handwriting on the back of a petrol-station receipt.

One word frees us of all the weight and pain of life. That word is love.

YOUR NOTES

....
....
....
....
....
....
....
....
....
....
....
....
....
....

YOUR NOTES

....
....
....
....
....
....
....
....
....
....
....
....
....
....
....

THE AFTER-PARTY

In most cases this means the evening party after the meal and speeches, but sometimes people hold the after-party on a different day, especially if they have married abroad with only a small group of family and friends in attendance.

It is not the quantity
of the meat, but
the cheerfulness of
the guests, which
makes the feast.

EDWARD HYDE

VENUE

There are several matters to think about and make decisions on when considering the venue of your after-party:

◆ Food – will you serve a buffet, snacks or a full meal?

◆ Music – disco, playlist or live band?

◆ Calling it a night – what time to conclude?

◆ Using the same venue makes logistics easier. However, if you are hosting an after-party in a separate place, book it a good time to ensure you can dovetail with your nuptials, and include directions between venues for guests.

Let us celebrate the
occasion with wine
and sweet words.

PLAUTUS

SIZE AND STYLE

◆ However much you might want to invite almost everyone you know to come along and celebrate with you, unless you have an extremely generous budget and a venue the size of Buckingham Palace, you will need to plot the guest list carefully.

◆ The after-party can have a theme or style all of its own, but the rule about not everyone loving fancy dress should still be observed!

◆ If you want a fun element, caricaturists and table magicians are universally popular.

FOOD

- Buffets are a great way of making sure that there is something for everyone.

- A fish-and-chip van provides novelty value as well as sustenance, as does an ice-cream van, which is also a great way of doing an informal pudding. Both make great photo opportunities.

- Cheese and fruit, with plenty of bread and crackers, is always a crowd-pleaser.

- Sausage or bacon butties (with veggie and vegan options) may be basic, but after a marathon bop to Abba, Queen and Take That, they will provide much-needed fuel.

DRINK

◆ Most people expect to pay for their drinks at a venue where there is a licensed bar, but make sure that the expectation is conveyed via your invitation so that guests come prepared.

◆ If you want to give people their first drink, sort this with your venue and have a maximum set amount agreed.

◆ If you are running your own cash bar (remember that a licence will have to be obtained from your local authority), try to buy your beer and wine on a sale or return basis.

◆ An evening party will include guests who are driving. Be sure to cater for them with a range of soft drinks, as well as non-alcoholic beer and wine.

◆ If people are dancing then they will appreciate jugs of iced water on their tables.

◆ For members of the wedding party who have been on the go since the early hours, a reviving cup of tea, herbal tisane or coffee may well be welcome as the evening draws on.

MUSIC

Everyone likes a dance after a wedding, and the after-party is the perfect opportunity. If you are booking a DJ, remember to ask:

- For testimonials/feedback
- What range of music they play
- If they can accommodate a requested playlist
- What equipment they have – lights, smoke machine, etc.
- What their fee is
- Where they will be travelling from (try to avoid booking anyone who has to travel too far and is therefore more likely to run into traffic problems).

Music is a moral law.
It gives a soul to the
universe, wings to
the mind, flight to
the imagination, a
charm to sadness and
life to everything.

ANONYMOUS

∽ DON'T FORGET ∽

Take some time in between the reception and the after-party for you and your partner to be alone together. A wedding day can be a whirlwind affair, but stealing away for half an hour gives you both a chance to share a special moment before you slip back into being the hosts with the most. Effectively, you will be pressing pause and remembering what this day is all about. THEN you can go and lead the 'Time Warp'! It's just a jump to the left…

DISASTER DODGER

With so much to think about in advance, it can be very easy to forget some of the more mundane 'after the party' essentials.

◆ Transport – home or honeymoon, don't forget to book a ride!

◆ Keys – if you need car/house keys, make sure that you have entrusted them to someone or have them safely stowed.

◆ Dignity – watch how much you drink across the course of the day. A bride or groom being carried out of their own wedding three sheets to the wind is not a good look.

Dare, dream, dance,
smile, and sing loudly!
And have faith that love
is an unstoppable force!

Suzanne Brockmann

YOUR NOTES

YOUR NOTES

....
....
....
....
....
....
....
....
....
....
....
....
....
....
....

THE HONEYMOON

Planning a wedding can be exhausting, and you're likely to be ready for a restorative break once the big day is done and dusted. Discuss destinations and budget, book ahead, and look forward to walking hand-in-hand into the sunset!

Come, let's be a
comfortable couple and
take care of each other...
How glad we shall be,
that we have somebody
we are fond of always,
to talk to and sit with.

CHARLES DICKENS

READY FOR THE 'OFF'

◆ Unless you're driving, remember to book transport to the airport or rail tickets. Ensure that you have all the required travel documents (ideally at least two weeks prior to departure).

◆ If leaving directly from your reception, make sure you have honeymoon luggage stored safely at your venue. Likewise, remember to hand over wedding outfits to friends or family for safekeeping before you depart.

◆ If you are leaving the next day, pack your cases before the wedding. This will give you time to catch your breath and prevent any frantic last-minute dashing about.

Here we stop.
On the threshold of
wedding nights stands
an angel smiling, a
finger to his lips.

VICTOR HUGO

HOME OR AWAY?

◆ The destination is entirely up to you, but if either time or money is in short supply, a honeymoon in your own country could be the ideal solution.

◆ Renting a cottage or apartment could be cheaper than a hotel, or might simply better suit your needs. Check out companies specialising in romantic properties.

◆ If travelling abroad, let the airline know this is your honeymoon. You might just get upgraded!

◆ Make sure you organise any inoculations and visas in good time, if travelling to countries where they are an entry requirement.

MINI-MOON

Some couples opt for a mini-moon – a short break instead of a full-blown holiday. Here are some ideas…

◆ A city break: Paris, New York, Madrid – the world is your oyster!

◆ A lazy weekend at a spa could be the perfect antidote to the manic pre-wedding organisation.

◆ One night in a top-notch hotel can make some special memories.

◆ Hire a campervan for a weekend and go wherever takes your fancy.

◆ Many glamping packages include a newlyweds' weekend. Starry nights for the starry-eyed!

BUDGET IDEAS

After the expense of a wedding, funds may be tight...

◆ Timing is everything: holidays booked either a long time in advance or very last minute can result in incredible deals. All-inclusive packages can also be extremely cost-effective, as you won't need much in the way of spending money.

◆ If you know anyone with a holiday home, ask if you can borrow it.

◆ Camping can be romantic AND economical. Look around for cities in pretty locations or on the outskirts of historic towns.

◆ Rental accommodation companies, like Airbnb, give you some glorious options at affordable prices all over the world, while rural pubs offering rooms deliver heavenly countryside with food and drink on tap.

◆ If you have friends or family living abroad, consider visiting them and combining your honeymoon with a trip to see your far-flung loved ones. If they can put you up then you can eliminate accommodation costs.

◆ Competitions to win a honeymoon are plentiful. Enter 'win a holiday' or 'win a honeymoon' into a search engine and try your luck!

✦ DON'T FORGET ✦

◆ If your passport is due to expire soon, you might need to renew it before travelling. Check the entry requirements of the country in question before booking.

◆ You can apply for a passport in your new name up to three months before your marriage or civil partnership. Your old passport will be cancelled and your new one is 'post-dated' (you can't use it before the ceremony).

◆ You don't need to change your passport if you are keeping your name.

DISASTER DODGER

◆ Check with your travel agent regarding their refund policy in event of cancellation on either side.

◆ When choosing the destination for your honeymoon, it is sensible to avoid places that have been recently affected by war or that look as if they may become embroiled in conflict. The Foreign Office website will advise you.

◆ Time any necessary vaccinations so that you won't be experiencing any side effects when you marry.

◆ Make sure that wedding presents are safely stored with family or friends in your absence, especially envelopes containing cash, cheques and vouchers.

Our honeymoon
will shine our life long:
its beams will only fade
over your grave or mine.

CHARLOTTE BRONTË

I have a fantastic husband. Here's the honeymoon part: I still think he's the funniest, wittiest, most clever man I've ever known.

Sarah Jessica Parker

YOUR NOTES

YOUR NOTES

....
....
....
....
....
....
....
....
....
....
....
....
....
....
....

AFTER THE WEDDING

It can feel a bit anticlimactic
after your big day, but a wedding
is the gift that keeps on giving.
There are photos to be selected,
presents to unwrap, thank
you cards to be written and
perhaps the video to watch.

No duty is more
urgent than that of
returning thanks.

JAMES ALLEN

THANK-YOU CARDS

◆ Handwritten, these should be done as soon as possible after the wedding, while the details are still fresh in your head.

◆ When thanking people for vouchers or money, explain what you intend to purchase – people like to know what they are contributing towards.

◆ Buy stationery in advance, or arrange to have an image uploaded and made into a note card immediately after the wedding.

◆ Include a special and heartfelt message to those who helped in any particular way. People really appreciate knowing that their contribution was valued.

◆ Don't forget to include your parents and close family in your written thank yous. Even if you see them every day, a special note expressing your love and gratitude will mean the world to them.

◆ If you are moving to a new house, combine thank-you cards with change-of-address cards to save on postage and another task.

◆ Use thank-you cards to remind people that you would love to see any photographs they may have taken.

SENDING WEDDING CAKE

◆ Not everyone bothers with this now, but tradition states that you should send a piece of cake to anyone who was invited but couldn't attend or to other people you wish to acknowledge.

◆ Don't cut the cake into slices until you are about to package it and mail it. This will help to keep it fresh and moist.

◆ If you are mailing cake, make sure you buy sturdy boxes made for the purpose and put these inside jiffy bags for extra protection against bumps and knocks.

- A paper napkin wrapped around the cake before boxing it will also provide additional protection in transit.

- If mailing cake abroad, be aware that some countries have restrictions on sending food through the post. Check with your local post office.

- When sending traditional wedding cake to pet owners, remember that raisins can make dogs very poorly. If Fido intercepts the post, you could have a sick pooch on your conscience. Check with the recipient before dispatching.

RETURNS AND REFUNDS

Be sure to return any hired clothing, accessories or equipment as soon as possible. If you're going away directly after the wedding, leave a list of returns with a friend and ask them to ensure that everything goes back to wherever it should, within the time frame specified. Ask them to get written acknowledgement of any returns – and don't forget to claim any deposits back.

The smallest act of
kindness is worth
more than the
grandest intention.

Oscar Wilde

DON'T FORGET

◆ Stock up on postage stamps before the wedding and invest in a couple of good-quality pens to write your missives.

◆ Thank people specifically: for their gift, for the part they played in your big day and for coming. If they travelled a significant distance, be sure to let them know how glad you are that they made the effort.

◆ If sending notes to elderly people or those who are sick and were unable to attend, include a few photographs so that they feel included and are aware that they were in your thoughts.

◆ A note to suppliers and service providers will be greatly appreciated. Where possible, provide a testimonial or complete the relevant feedback form.

◆ If a member of staff of any organisation who was part of your wedding really excelled, take the time to write to their superiors and tell them. This could be genuinely beneficial to the individual and could earn you a gift voucher for your trouble.

◆ Likewise, address any glitches or disappointing service issues as soon as possible after the wedding. Be specific and insistent.

In all the wedding cake,
hope is the sweetest
of the plums.

Douglas Jerrold

DISASTER
DODGER

If you run short of cake, don't panic! Most supermarkets sell excellent basic wedding cakes – or plain white-iced fruit cakes – and it is, after all, the thought that counts. Besides, nobody but you and your spouse will ever know that the cake landing on doormats is any different to the confection you cut on your wedding day. Shh!

Grow old along with me.
The best is yet to be...

ROBERT BROWNING

YOUR NOTES

....

....

....

....

....

....

....

....

....

....

....

....

....

....

....

YOUR NOTES

....
....
....
....
....
....
....
....
....
....
....
....
....
....

CONCLUSION:

The ten golden rules of
wedding planning

◆ Don't feel obliged to follow tradition or to
please others.

◆ If you find yourself getting stressed by endless
planning, take a deep breath and share
the load.

◆ Plan ahead and make sure to have contingency
arrangements in place where you can. If your
organisational skills are flaky, consider using a
wedding planner.

◆ Preparing for your wedding should be fun.
Remember to make memories to treasure as
well as lists.

- Keep it personal. Add small touches and references that really mean something. Write your own vows or wear a piece of your granny's jewellery, for example.

- A good night's sleep will present you at your radiant best. Whether it's lavender on your pillow or reading your tax return, embrace whatever sends you to the land of Nod.

- Ring-fence time with your beloved that is wedding-talk-free.

- Keep your temper and your sense of humour.

- Accept that some things are beyond your control – and that marrying your beloved is ultimately all that truly matters.

- Smile! Set your mouth to full beam and enjoy every second of your wedding planning.

If you're interested in finding out more about our books find us on Facebook at **Summersdale Publishers** and follow us on Twitter at **@Summersdale**.

www.summersdale.com